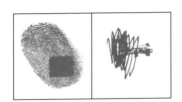

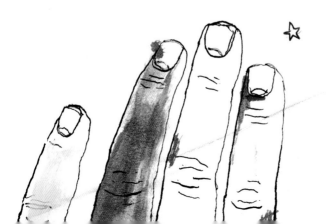

My name
is Jason.

Mine too.

OUR STORY.

OUR WAY.

# by
# Jason
# Reynolds
# and
# Jason
# Griffin

Atheneum

NEW YORK   LONDON   TORONTO
SYDNEY   NEW DELHI

A very special shout-out of thanks
goes to Joanna Cutler, Alyson Day,
Karen Nagel, Lydia Wills, Jason
Yarn, Charles Yuen, Carla Weise,
Ruiko Tokunaga, Dorothy Pietrewicz,
Christopher Baily, Jenny Rozbruch,
and Kathryn Silsand.

ATHENEUM BOOKS FOR YOUNG READERS
An imprint of Simon & Schuster Children's Publishing Division
1230 Avenue of the Americas, New York, New York 10020
This work is a memoir. It reflects the author's present recollections of
his experiences over a period of years.

For information about special discounts for bulk purchases, please
contact Simon & Schuster Special Sales at 1-866-506-1949 or
business@simonandschuster.com.
The Simon & Schuster Speakers Bureau can bring authors to your live
event. For more information or to book an event, contact the Simon &
Schuster Speakers Bureau at 1-866-248-3049 or visit our website at
www.simonspeakers.com.
Also available in an Atheneum Books for Young Readers hardcover edition
The illustrations for this book were rendered in various physical and
digital media.
Manufactured in China
First Atheneum Books for Young Readers paperback edition June 2022
10  9  8  7  6  5  4  3  2  1
Library of Congress Cataloging-in-Publication Data
Names: Reynolds, Jason, author. | Griffin, Jason, illustrator.
Title: My name is Jason. Mine too : our story, our way / Jason
Reynolds ; illustrated by Jason Griffin.
Description: New York : Atheneum Books for Young Readers 2022. |
"This work is a memoir. It reflects the authors present recollections
of his experiences over a period of years."—Copyright page. | Audience:
Ages 12 and Up | Audience: Grades 7-9 | Summary: "Jason Reynolds.
Jason Griffin. One a poet. One an artist. One Black. One white. Two
voices. One journey. To move to New York, and make it in New York.
Best friends willing to have a hard life if it meant a happy life.
All they needed was a chance. A reissue of a memoir of a moment in time
within a lifetime of friendship"—Provided by publisher.
Identifiers: LCCN 2021049639 (print) | LCCN 2021049640 (ebook) |
ISBN 9781534478237 (hardcover) | ISBN 9781534478220 (paperback) |
ISBN 9781534478244 (ebook)
Classification: LCC PS3618.E9753 M9 2022 (print) |
LCC PS3618.E9753 (ebook) | DDC 811/.6—dc23
LC record available at https://lccn.loc.gov/2021049639
LC ebook record available at https://lccn.loc.gov/2021049640

A poet. An artist. Black. White. We were college roommates. Now, close friends.

I could taste graduation. Tasted like freedom. No clue of what to do with that freedom. Worked at a bookstore. At the checkout counter I wrote poems.

Dropped out of school. felt like freedom . I was a business major but only took art classes. I just wanted to paint. Without the lecture. So I left and I did. With all the free time, I started working with Jason. I did the art. He wrote drafts of poems at work.

At night we met at Jason's house. I shared my poems. He shared his paintings. we shared similar pain, similar happiness, similar fear. We made the poems and paintings share space, just as we'd learned to.

A poet. An artist. Black. White. SELF .

Not SELVES. SELF.

I wasn't quite satisfied. Needed room to grow . Decided to move to New York City. Figured it would be easier to make it there with a friend, so I asked Jason to come. Idea: sell SELF there.

I felt like a second grader. Like if I said no he wouldn't be my friend anymore. Started packing my bags. Had to tell my mom. She loathes New York.

I was glad he said yes. I knew he was **nervous** about it. I insisted.

The ride seemed to last forever. Didn't think we'd ever get there. Secretly, I hoped we'd never get there.

New home. New hope. **Brooklyn**. Beautiful Bed-Stuy. A plastic plant, a wicker couch, a couple of mattresses, and boxes upon boxes of books.

And a **TV**. The one we had in college.

No sweat.

Shortly after arriving we learned the rules. **No money**. **No name**. **No chance**.

No food. For the first six months we only ate cereal, peanut butter toast.

Tuna. **Fried tuna**. Tuna and rice. Rice and soup.

The hungrier we got, the closer we became. Within months we were family. **Brothers**.

**Forced to lean** on each other.

Couldn't afford not to.

Couldn't afford canvas. Jason painted on abandoned wooden doors, old checkbooks, milk cartons, and whatever else he could find. **Visitors, beware**.

Jason sat in the window of a coffee shop every single day for about three months, writing a collection of poems. Poems about friendship, growth, creativity. He drank coffee.

**Lots of coffee.**

It was time to take a huge risk. If I failed, at least Jason would be there to fail with me. I had an art show.

**My mom got sick. I live in New York. I never should've left home.**

Hundreds of people came to the show.

**Really cool people. Jason's mom was there. She asked about my mother. I said she was fine. I lied.**

I didn't sell a single piece. A failure.
**Men pretend not to cry. I did. Rent's due.**

**All those people came to see Jason's work. A success. My mother sent her love from the hospital.**

Rent's late. There's always something.

**So tired. So worried. So many questions. I needed to write.**

Somehow I had to make it work. Somehow we had to make it work. I hoped.

what do people think of us? what are we being perceived as? irresponsible or passionate? probably stupid.

why be an artist? was dropping out of school a bad decision? should I hang up the brush? why are my clothes too big?

why do we care? I'm having the time of my life. good times. bad times. never laughed so loud. never cried so hard. never actually thought risks were worth it. changed my mind. let's make a book. I'll start writing now.

Rent's paid. Again. we always seem to make it. They never seem to understand us. that's ok. They never seem to stop us either.

A poet. An artist. black. white. regular guys. survivors. friends. brothers.

pretty cool.

By the way, to all those reading, my name is jason.

Mine too.

Nervous

TEN

Pro bab We ME
Shared

☑ NO NAME

My name is Jason

WHY
BE AN TOO
ARTIST BIG
BROOKLYN
se

SICK

CHANCE
BROTHER

AAAAAAAAAAAAAAA
POET
POET
POET
POET
POET
POET
POET
POET
POET

reading

No money

SOMETHING

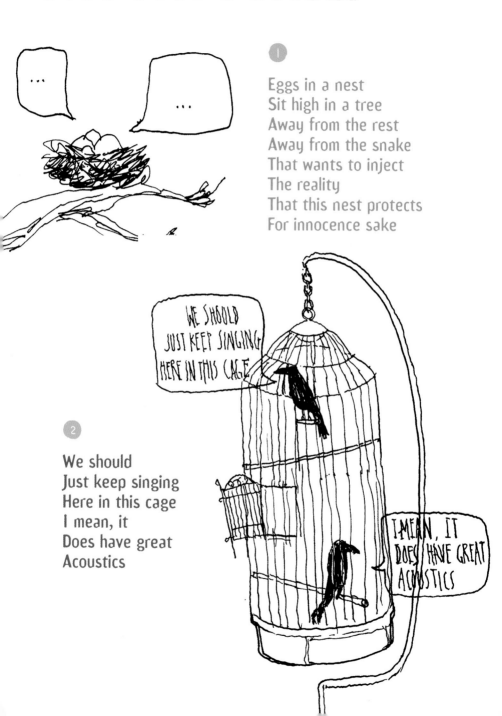

1

Eggs in a nest
Sit high in a tree
Away from the rest
Away from the snake
That wants to inject
The reality
That this nest protects
For innocence sake

2

We should
Just keep singing
Here in this cage
I mean, it
Does have great
Acoustics

3

The early bird
Don't necessarily
Always catch
The worm
It just be
The first awake
To recognize
It's hungry
Should've slept in

4

An Epiphany:
There's gotta be
More
Than just cages
And worms
I gotta have wings
For a reason
I gotta have

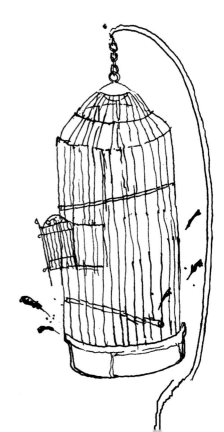

FELT

LIKE

FREEDOM

A straight A
Student
Who stepped in
Front of
A train

Crushed
With a
Capital C

A straight A
Student
Who stepped in
Front of
A train

Crushed
With a
Capital C

use fork

Father a daughter
walking

Father a daughter
walking

I don't know when we were tied together
Intertwined in invisible rope
Two puppets that move without a master
Two dummies who find their lives in laughter
Two men who fear the same disaster
And share in the same hope

SELF

art?

Here
Today
We change

Meet me at the
Railroad tracks
Bring your art supplies
And an extra handful
Of courage
Just in case the
Trains come

Just in case
Yesterday decides
To show its face

We'll create a piece of art
To bring forth peace of heart
And tell grandparents
With hate-stained memories
To hold on to hope
For healing can happen
Before heaven

art.

Here
Today
We stand

At the train tracks
That separate different
Parts of the same land

Paint and pen in hand
Feet planted on a
Ground now common
Praying painting poeting that blood
On this ground
Won't be

Anymore

nervous

Through the rearview
My house shrinks
My heart sinks
To the bottom
Of a spoiled
Stomach

I'm afraid
I'll miss dinner tonight
Mom

But I had to go
Find my appetite

~~Decided to move~~

~~to borough~~

~~to borough crowde~~

Decided to move
to borough   crowded with dreams.
hope there's room for mine

BROOKLYN.

I was warned about this city
Told the tales of torturous time
A painful paradise for the unpretty
A week of work is worth a dime

Told to fear this savage land
If I desired my life spared
Give not and take not a hand
Sensitivity never shared

I have heard the rumors ring
Every person lives a lie
On the train don't say a thing
Look nobody in the eye

But I've learned
Ain't no heaven in this city
If all you do is hide

# no money

Monday morning

I promised

My pants pockets

A love connection soon

A nice nickel

A dime divine

A dollar dream to swoon

But I know how these pockets do

They never change, it's nothing new

This love connection will be through

By Tuesday afternoon

Sometimes I like to
Take taxis
To wherever the cool
People hang out
And get out
Wearing a huge hat
Sunglasses
And a scarf around
My mouth

I can see a child
Outside my window
Sitting on the
Concrete shore
With feet in an
Asphalt sea
cRying
Fighting against the
Current

Pulling
Pulling him in

No chance

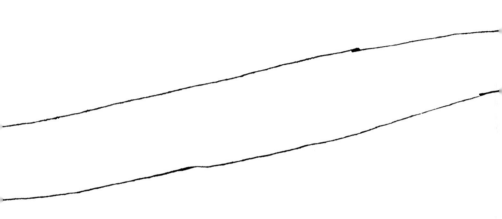

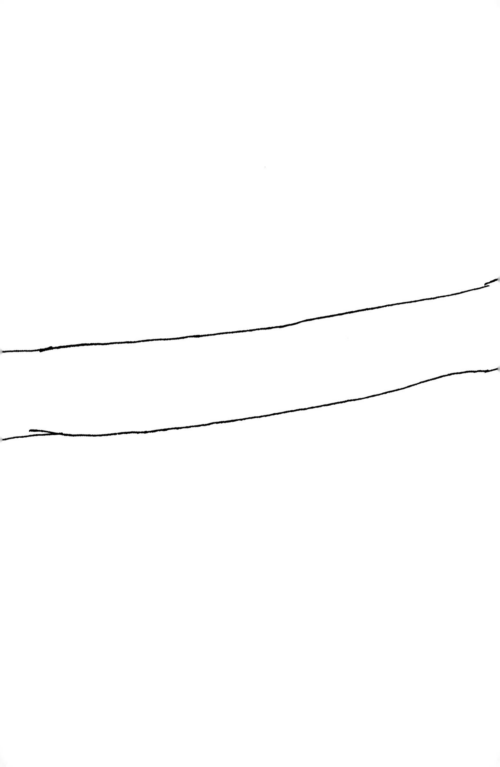

# fried tuna

SALTY SOUP
SAME SANDWICH FROM
ON ~~SUNDAY~~ SATURDAY
SOGGY CEREAL
SELDOM SWEET

LIFE IS HILARIOUS
A RIOT TO EAT RICE
AND SACRIFICE

REAL FOOD
FOR HEAT

SUNDAY
~~SATURDAY~~

THE

ARTØST

in take
two

THE
ARTIST

No 200

PAINT

R&G

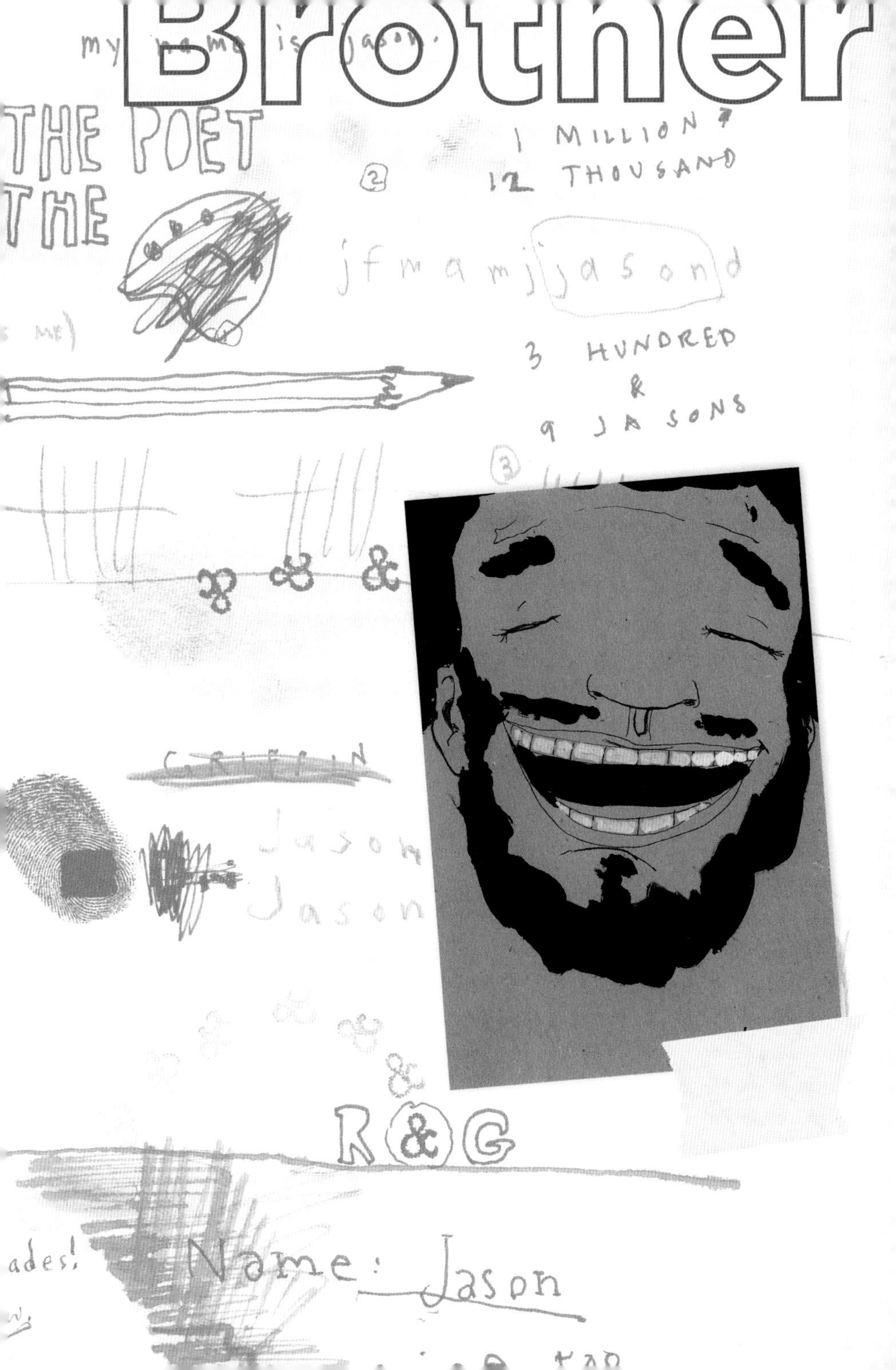

# Brother

THE POET
THE
(s Me)

my name is Jason

② 1 MILLION ₱
12 THOUSAND

jfnamj jasond

3 HUNDRED
&
9 JASONS

③

& & &

GRIFFIN

Jason
Jason

& &

&

R & G

ades!

Name: Jason

I gotta friend whose hair is red
Looks like a fire atop his head

Mine is curly, thick and black
Pay it no mind I like it like that

And if anyone ever asks me why
I choose to hang out with this guy
I'll say we're different yes I know
But for us both hair does grow
So-and-so can carry on
For we'll be friends
                    till hair is gone

THIS WAS SUPPOSED TO BE
A CLICHÉD P O E M
ABOUT CLIMBING THE MOUNTAIN
OF LIFE ON MY OWN

BUT WHEN I SAT DOWN TO WRITE IT
I REALIZED T H A T
I HAD TO ASK A FRIEND OF MINE
FOR A PIECE OF PAPER

**Forced to lean**

# Visitors, beware

There's a guy on our couch

And a sink full of dishes

Hot water on the stove

And a fridge full of wishes


And paint has spilled all over

The kitchen floor


There's a stain on the rug

And a splat on the wall

And a half bag of chips

That is shared by us all


So it's funny to request

That each and every guest

Take their shoes off at the door

A BLACK BIRD LANDS AND TAKES A REST

FROM FLYING SO FREE

A YELLOW BIRD FROZEN

LIKE A VASE ON A SHELF

AFRAID TO FLY

A BLUE BIRD SAD WITH BROKEN WINGS

HAS FALLEN FROM A TREE

AND A RED BIRD WITH SO MUCH PASSION TO FLY

A RED BIRD KINDA LIKE ME

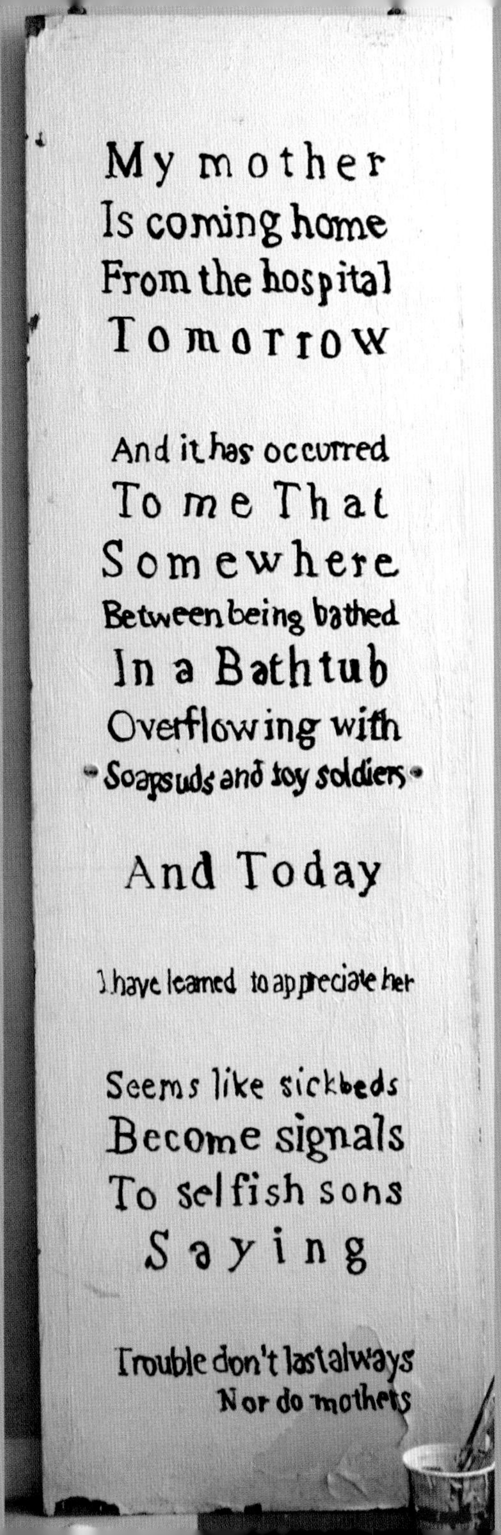

My mother
Is coming home
From the hospital
Tomorrow

And it has occurred
To me That
Somewhere
Between being bathed
In a Bathtub
Overflowing with
Soapsuds and toy soldiers

And Today

I have learned to appreciate her

Seems like sickbeds
Become signals
To selfish sons
Saying

Trouble don't last always
Nor do mothers

**really cool people**

chyanne

used to teach kindergarten

jealous of four-year-olds'

stick figures

made with crayon

on construction paper

she cried at their

creativity

and quit to become

a copycat

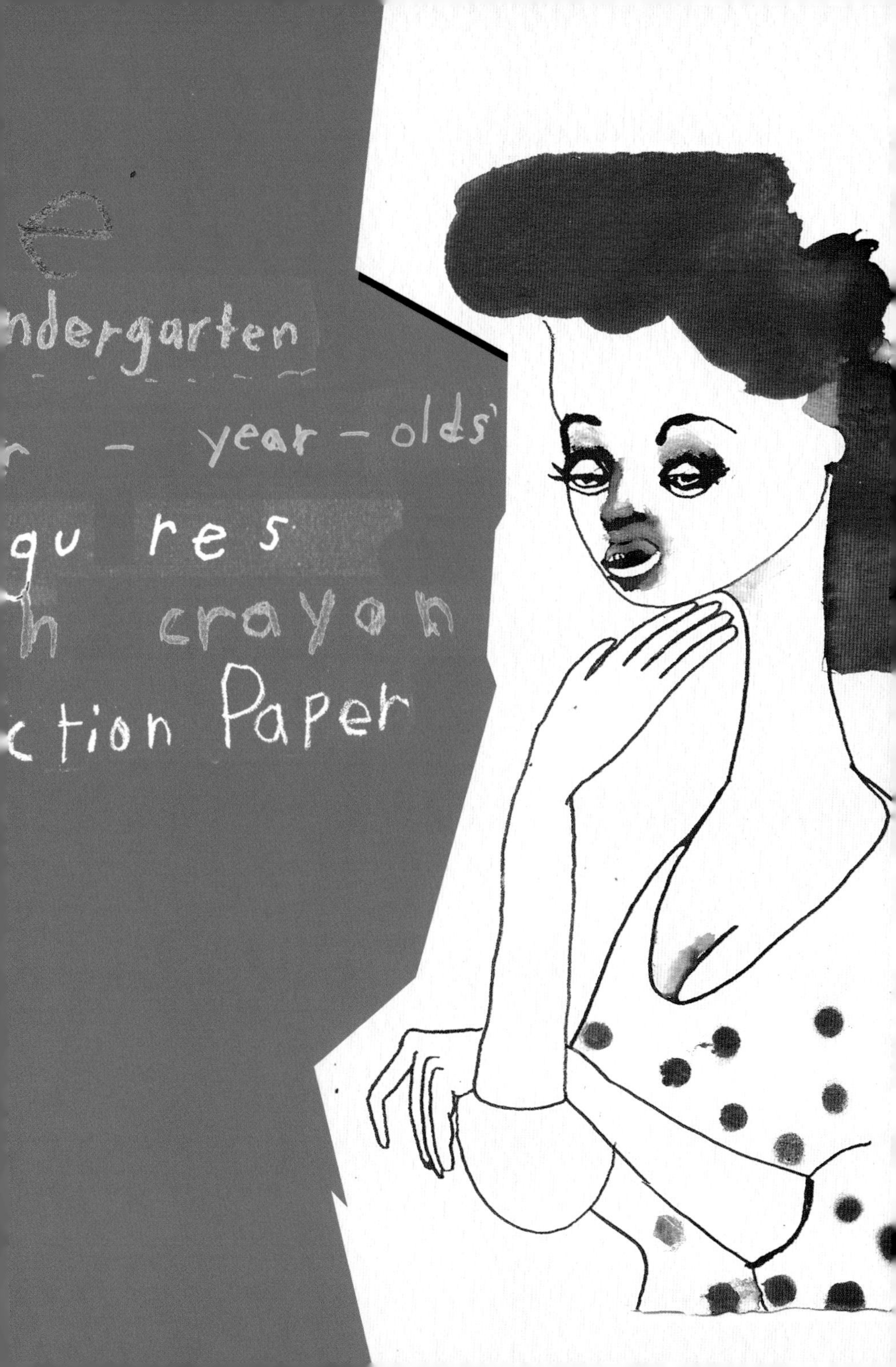

really
cool
people

EARNEST Ernest ERNEST ERNEST

Ernest

ERNEST

WAS IN THE DRAMA CLUB
in high school
LAUGHED AT
when the principal
APPLAUDED HIS PERFORMANCE
During morning
ANNOUNCEMENTS

saw him the other day
Wearing clothes
SIMILAR TO THE ONES
HE WORE THEN

I wanted to speak
But I know billboards
DON'T SPEAK BACK

# Franco

really
cool
people

IN HIS TWENTIES
HE WAS SELLING
HOTDOGS TO
TOURISTS

FOUR FOR A FRANK
FIVE ~~——~~ WITH A BUN

~~IN HIS THIRTIES~~

IN HIS THIRTIES
HE WROTE A BOOK
~~ABOUT~~ ABOUT IT

*Franks by Frank*

SOLD A MILLION COPIES

IN HIS FORTIES
HE USED THE MONEY
TO BUY ART
REALLY
REALLY
REALLY
EXPENSIVE ART

~~NOW HE'S IN HIS~~

NOW HE'S IN HIS FIFTIES
AND THIS IS THE STORY
HE TELLS

Men don't cry
or write poetry
or paint
or dance
or hug
or kiss
or like
or love
or listen
I hear

I guess they pretend

There's something there
Something I have always had
Complicated and complex
Turn my happiness to sad
Keeping me from what is next

There's something there
Whispering in an open ear
Telling me to be afraid
When I sleep it reappears
Mashing up the things I've made

There's something there
With its hand around my heart
Squeezing till it does not beat
Stopping me before I start
Comfortable within defeat

There's something there
Something there I can't ignore
But I don't want it there for sure
For something there must leave
Before It scars me till my soul is sore

And I never get to something more

There's something there
Something I have always had
Complicated and complex
Turn my happiness to sad
Keeping me from what is next

There's something there
Whispering in an open ear
Telling me to be afraid
When I sleep it reappears
Mashing up the things I've made

There's something there
With its hand around my heart
Squeezing me till it does not beat
Stopping me before I start
Comfortable within defeat

There's something there
Something there I can't ignore
But I don't want it there for sure
For something there must leave
Before it scares me till my soul is sore
And I never get to something more

It's hard to walk
With my pants
Falling down
Saggin'

Blue jeans
With deep
Pockets packed
With pain

I just need
A moment

Some time
To rest

A moment
To pull
Out the
Poems

If you can't eat the poem
And you can't drink the paint
Then a dummy you are
And an artist you ain't

Call me when you grow up
Or when you blow up

Whichever happens first

I LOVE YOU LOSER

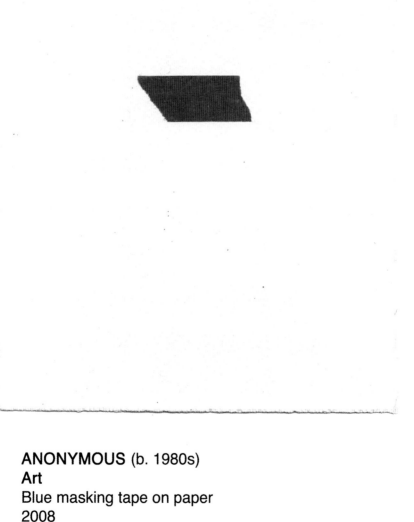

**ANONYMOUS** (b. 1980s)
**Art**
Blue masking tape on paper
2008
$100,000 – $150,000

I'd like to think ~~my~~
my poems are like
picnic potato chips.

Lightly salted slices of
heaven.

But there are always a few
burnt ones in the bag.

This is one of those.

# Why be an artist?

too

New York has
Finally offered me
Importance

A gift I guess

Something nice to wear
To the totem pole party

Of course, I accepted it
But I refuse to wear it
Instead I gave it to
My mother

Why do we care?

Told her keep it
By her bed
By the picture of me
Framed in humility
For the nights
When she questions

Whether or not
This city is
Swallowing me whole

$\mathcal{L}$ife is good

life: Good
life: Good
life: Good

life: Good

That's OK

If there
was only
a drop in
the glass

no more

I'd be

A little

Less thirsty

Than I was

Before

It's so hard
To explain to people
The beauty in brokenness
The scarring in sweet salvation
The lovely lacerations
Of the unlimited
Unlaminated
Illuminated
Few
Who dare to do don'ts
Miss a few meals
But will to do won'ts
While well-to-dos
Whisper questions
Regarding
Who I think I am
And who they think
I should be

I laugh and hope
They leave
Me alone

Because it's just
So hard
To explain to people
That my life
Is not unhard
But not unhappy

He walks in
His hair everywhere
His clothes not so neat
But he's comfortable and
He's confident

He walks in
Books in his hand
Words running around
His mind like children
Playing tag on a snow day
He's ready

He walks in
Introduces himself as a poet
And their professor

Each student wondering
Where his corduroy blazer was
Where his horn-rimmed glasses
And corncob pipe were
And when was his beard
Going to turn white

He walks in
As himself and
Teaches his first lesson
On cliché

A poet

I wrote a poem once
About a poem that could
Do things

Like grow legs and walk
Grow arms and hold someone
Wrap them in wonderfuls
And other good words

A poem with a heart

A poem that could
Jump rope on the sidewalk
And high five
Five-year-olds for
Smiling and laughing

A poem that could smile
And laugh
And listen
To old ladies talk

About the poems
They're sick and tired of

A poem that could live forever
And give birth
To humans

And tell them how
Great they are

A poem with
No comma
Period
Or indentation
That could love
And love

I wrote a poem once
About a poem that could
Do things

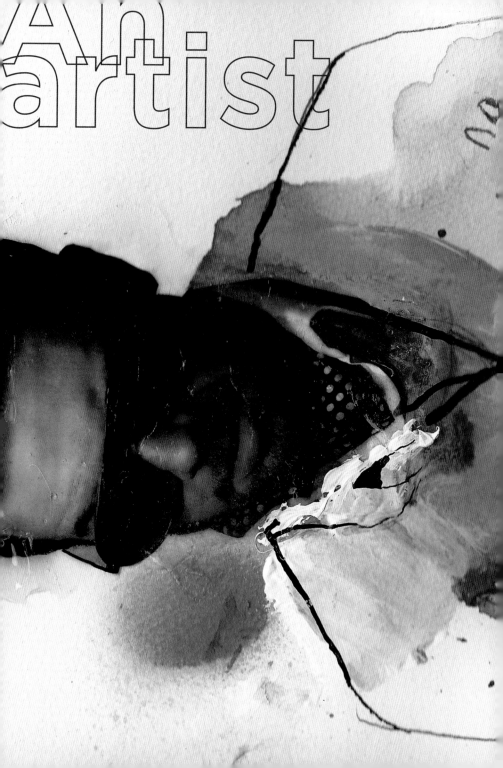

There's paint on every pot and pan
On every spoon, fork and knife
There's paint on everything he's touched
And every moment of his life

Question to a Friend

What happens if the pen runs dry
And the canvas doesn't stretch
Or if there was no more paper supply
And pencils didn't sketch?

What if my hands suddenly were numb
And there was nothing I could hold
Or if suddenly I was deaf and dumb
And no story could be told?

What if all I could paint was the color black
And the only word I could write was wrong?
What if my niche just wasn't my knack
And I was misled all along?

What if painting was a sin
And poetry became taboo
And no one ever clapped for me again
My question is, would you?

to all those reading

# MY NAME IS JASON

mine too.

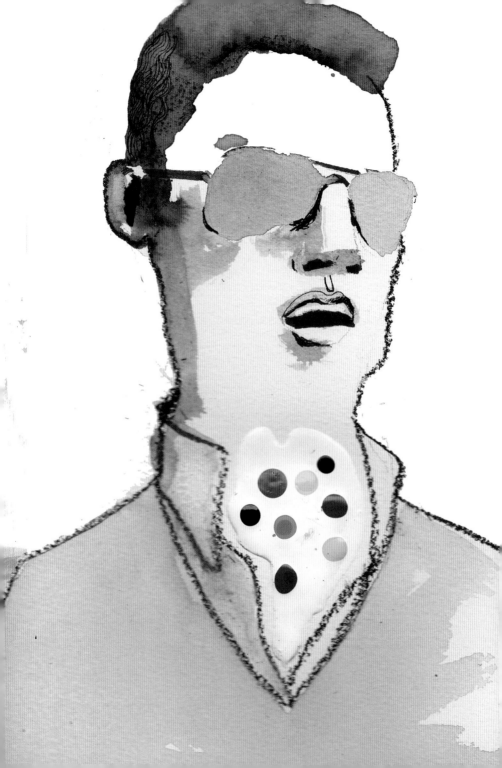

# Thirteen years later...

**Griffin:** Thinking back, over a decade ago, when we were creating *My Name Is Jason. Mine Too.*, what memory stands out to you?

**Reynolds:** The fact that we seemed to never sleep! Seriously, when I think back, I remember the two of us moving to Brooklyn, unpacking everything—which wasn't much—and then eating Chinese food. After that . . . work. Just, work! I'd go to bed at like three a.m., leaving you awake painting on old doors we found on the street or whatever else you could get your hands on. I'd wake up and come downstairs at nine a.m., and you'd already be up, sitting on the floor in the kitchen, working. It was almost as if you never went to sleep. Like you were a machine!

**Griffin:** Man, just thinking about that schedule makes me tired! But I appreciate that, J, especially coming from one of the hardest-working people I know. It's kinda cliché, but when you're doing what you love, it doesn't feel like work. That being said, I think there was also a bit of fear driving us. Or maybe the balancing act of ego and humility. Moving to the big city, and quickly realizing the big city wasn't waiting for us, definitely stands out as a moment. The work in this book reminds me of how we coped with that reality. And also how we were willing to bet it all because we felt we had no other choice. Like, *This is our shot—we can't slip up.*

**Reynolds:** There was definitely some fear there. And definitely a peculiar ego at that age. I was twenty. You were twenty-two. We really believed we were making something no one had ever seen and that we were reinventing what people thought of when they thought of books. I'm not sure we completely succeeded, and honestly, looking back, I'm not sure that even matters. But it definitely meant something that we wanted to push ourselves that way. That we were able to harness the moxie of youth to make whatever we wanted.

Now we're almost twenty years older. Do you still feel that?

**Griffin:** Good point. And that's such an interesting question. For me, I think it's always about truth—but how we find that truth is a different story. And so if truth is the barometer, then in some ways I have to work harder now. It's almost like it becomes harder to be honest, and I have to purposely unlearn certain things to get to it. Such a strange concept. But a great example of how we, adults, need to stop and thank our younger selves, and learn from them. And in some ways, strive to be them.

**Reynolds:** I totally agree. Because I miss the Jason that wrote this book. Well, actually, that's not true. I hunt that Jason down every morning to continue this work. And not just the work of making art, because this book ain't even about that. But the work of being a friend to myself, and a friend to others.

**Griffin:** And perhaps that requires exactly what it required back then—working through emotional layers of excitement, insecurity, hope, to name a few. Laughter definitely got us through too. Remember that time I tried to hurdle the spiked iron fence?

**Reynolds:** Of course! You remember crashing parties just for food?

**Griffin:** Yooooo, that's right! Destroying the refreshments. You know how many little plates you gotta eat to get full?! They knew, bro. They all knew.

**Reynolds:** They definitely knew! But we did whatever it took. And twenty years later, though differently, we're still doing whatever it takes.

**Griffin:** Some things never change.

—November 202